Let Us Pray

Let Us Pray

Contemporary Prayers for the Seasons of the Church

ISRAEL GALINDO

Judson Press

Valley Forge

Let Us Pray: Contemporary Prayers for the Seasons of the Church
© 1999 by Judson Press, Valley Forge, PA 19482-0851

Library of Congress Cataloging-in-Publication Data

Galindo, Israel.
    Let us pray : contemporary prayers for the seasons of the church /
Israel Galindo.
        p. cm.
    Includes bibliographical references and index.
    ISBN 0-8170-1296-6 (pbk. : alk. paper).
    1. Church year – Prayer-books and devotions – English. 2. Baptists –
Prayer-books and devotions – English. 3. Pastoral prayers.
    I. Title.
    BV30.G35 1999
    264'.13 – dc21   98-43237

Printed in the U.S.A.
06   05   04   03   02   01   00   99
5   4   3   2   1

BUSINESS REPLY MAIL

FIRST-CLASS MAIL   PERMIT NO. 6   VALLEY FORGE PA

POSTAGE WILL BE PAID BY ADDRESSEE

JUDSON PRESS

PO BOX 851

VALLEY FORGE PA 19482-9897

Book title: _____

Your comments: _____

Where did you hear about this book: _____

Reasons why you bought this book: (check all that apply) ☐ Subject ☐ Author ☐ Attractive Cover
☐ Recomendation of a friend ☐ Recomendation of a Reviewer ☐ Gift ☐ Other _____

If purchased: Bookseller _____ City _____ State _____

Please send me a Judson Press catalog. I am particularly interested in: (check all that apply)

1. ☐ African American
2. ☐ Baptist History/Beliefs
3. ☐ Bible Study
4. ☐ Children's Books
5. ☐ Christian Education
6. ☐ Christian Living
7. ☐ Church Leadership
8. ☐ Church Supplies
9. ☐ Devotional/Prayer
10. ☐ Preaching/Sermon Helps
11. ☐ Self-Help
12. ☐ Women's Issues

Yes, add my name to your mailing list!

Name (print) _____ Phone _____

Street _____

City _____ State _____ Zip _____

Please send a Judson Press catalog to my friend:

Name (print) _____ Phone _____

Street _____

City _____ State _____ Zip _____

To my friends and colleagues in ministry,
fellow pilgrims all,
and faithful companions
on the inner way:

Judy Bennett	Mike Harton
Steve Booth	Allen Jackson
Tim Brock	Terry Maples
Bob Dibble	Mark Price
David Fox	Mary Wrye

Contents

Part Four
PRAYERS FOR SPECIAL OCCASIONS

Introduction

Prayer is the most sacred and unique function of the Christian church; it has been called the soul of worship, and corporate prayer has been called the heart of corporate worship.[1] Simply put, corporate prayer is the joining of the hearts and minds of the people of God — the church — in praise, confession, and intercession.

It is tragic, therefore, that in contemporary worship corporate prayer seems more often than not a "filler" in the worship experience — or worse, it has become a mental nap time, a respite between other components of corporate worship.

Although this is a disappointing reality, it is understandable how things might have gotten this way. In some traditions, the only "real" prayer is extemporaneous — from the heart, led by the Spirit. Unfortunately, extemporaneous prayers are often unimaginative, repetitive, and lacking in the very elements most desired: a feeling of personal passion and connectedness with God and the congregation. Frank Segler warned that "where public prayer is undisciplined, corporate worship is in danger of decay."[2] Other traditions prefer written prayers, and there are several accepted sources for them. But those tend to sound pontifical and almost sanctimonious to the ear of the contemporary worshiper. Some worship leaders write their own prayers for corporate worship, and this is positive because it gives corporate prayer the attention it deserves in the formal worship experience. However, few of us are poets, and in the press of time and circumstances, the right words often are hard to come by. It is difficult to reveal both the mind of God and the heart of the people through prayer. Yet, this is what corporate prayer should do — and this is what we yearn to hear in our corporate worship experience.

Using the framework of the Christian Year, this book offers original contemporary prayers for each season as well as for special occasions. The value of using the Christian Year as a framework for corporate worship is being embraced even among non-liturgical churches. The natural structure of the Christian Year gives full expression to the Christian faith. It helps maintain a balanced teaching of cornerstone doctrines while keeping the worship of God focused on the revelation of God through the words and works of Jesus Christ. It is our hope that this collection of corporate prayers will be a resource for those who want to make the prayer components of corporate worship a more central and meaningful experience.

Notes

1. George Buttrick, *Prayer* (Nashville: Abingdon-Cokesbury Press, 1942), p. 283.

2. Franklin M. Segler, *Christian Worship: Its Theology and Practice* (Nashville: Broadman Press, 1967), p. 117. Used by permission.

Part One

ADVENT, CHRISTMAS, AND EPIPHANY PRAYERS

T HE FIRST CYCLE of the Christian Year consists of Advent, Christmas, and Epiphany. Advent, which begins the fourth Sunday before Christmas Day, marks the beginning of the Christian Year and bears witness to the coming of Christ, the promised Messiah. The mood of this season is joyful anticipation. The preparatory season of Advent culminates in the celebration of the Nativity of the Christ on Christmas Day.

Epiphany begins on January 6, twelve days after Christmas Day. This feast day commemorates the manifestation of Christ to the Gentiles. The story of the visit of the Magi is closely linked to this season. This part of the first cycle in the Christian Year emphasizes the realization of the gospel's global impact upon all nations, races, and peoples.

ADVENT

OUR GOD OF ADVENT,
in the midst of our preparations for Christmas —
    the tree, the decorations, the parties, the gifts —
    we are pressed to do it all before that deadline,
    December the twenty-fifth.

And while our preparations are hectic,
    we delight in the activity and color and sounds,
    for they distract us from the common time
    and remind us that some things about life
        are extraordinary:
like the wonder of children's imaginations;
the anticipated joy of surprises — received and given;
the reliving of the seasons in our lives,
        ever the same, ever changing;
    remembering good friends and family who have left us;
    and rejoicing in new friends
    and new family — through the bond of vows
        or the miracle of newborn life.

But in the midst of our Advent preparations,
    O God, give us longing hearts as reminders
    of the deeper mysteries of this season:
    the anticipation of the coming Child King
        who delivers us from the bondage of both law and sin
        and redeems through the power
            of humility and submission,
        who brings the knowledge of God
            into our hearts through the gift of his love,
for it is in his royal name we pray.
Amen.

Our God,
you whose promises are sure and secure,
we enter into this season of disciplined anticipation
    with the disadvantage of the knowledge of the outcome —
    we *know* how *this* familiar story will turn out.

Our God of Advent,
we confess that mysteries seem a thing of the past in our lives;
even children who once made wish lists in timid hope,
    today leave marked-up glossy catalogs
    as nonsubtle hints of implied good behavior.
With no mysteries under the tree,
they, too, have lost the mystery of anticipation,
    we fear.

In our hurried lives, we *need* the gift of anticipation,
    for we have lost the ability to wait,
    to cherish the moment,
    to embrace uncertainty
        and so, often, to live by faith.

We crave certitude, our God,
    in uncertain times;
    in the fear of threats to body and spirit
    we crave answers and solutions.
But you give us mysteries,
    angel visitations,
    and ask us to wait for "that day."

And so we ask for the gift of wondrous anticipation,
    that we may believe and live
    in the humble spirit of a young girl

given a gift, whispered a mystery,
and told to wait for God to act, *in that day.*

In this Advent season, our God,
give us this gift, that we too may see
your mysteries unfold in *our* lives.
For we pray in the name of the Christ Child
who is our Savior,
Jesus Christ.
Amen.

WE ARE TEMPTED, LORD,
to fret about the little things this season:
the shopping frenzy we will endure,
the gift list that isn't finished;
the party is coming up too quickly,
and the shopping days left till Christmas
are already growing fewer.
But we have heard the words of your prophet:
"Prepare the way of the Lord."
So we have come here to get ready for your arrival.
Help us to get ready, our God.
Help us to prepare for your coming
so that when you arrive
we might receive you,
worship and praise you —
for you alone are worthy of worship.
Amen.

OUR GOD, GIVER OF LIGHT,
we light these candles in this Advent season
    as a beacon against the darkness of our world.
With their lighting we announce
    the coming of the light in your Son,
he who himself was the light,
    and he whom the darkness of this world
    could not overcome.
With our voices we sing of your message of love.
With our music we celebrate the gift of salvation
    packaged in the body of a baby,
    entrusted to the humble care of two young people
    who could not know,
        could not *possibly* know,
that they held our destiny in their inexperienced arms.

Our Father of light,
you who have made yourself known
    through angels and babies,
enjoy our offering of worship today.
Delight in the voices of your children,
    accept the gifts we bring,
    for with these we confess that you are our God,
    who brought light into our lives
        and cast the darkness away.
Amen.

Our God,
we have heard the voice of your prophet,
sent as a herald of Good News.
 We are to prepare a way for the coming
  of our long-awaited Savior.
 We are to remove the obstacles in our lives
  that would hinder his coming to us.

And so we pray that in your Spirit, you would help us
 to cast away the doubts born of disappointments,
  that we may receive the Savior in faith;
 to cast off the mantle of self-sufficiency,
  that we may receive him humbly;
 and to cast away the pride borne of knowledge and familiarity,
  that we may be open to the mysteries of this Advent,
 so that this year, the Savior may come to us,
  not in the expected and anticipated ways
   of our own making,
  but in the wonder and mystery
   of your love for us.
Amen.

OUR HEAVENLY FATHER,
we're getting ready for Christmas.

The Christmas tree is up,
the wreath is hung on the door;
the ornaments are unboxed and in their places,
 reviving warm feelings of home and hearth
 and bringing welcomed memories of Christmases past.

The stockings are hung over the fireplace,
 the Christmas cards are getting out,
 and we're almost halfway through our shopping list.
We like to gripe, Lord,
 about the inconveniences of Christmastime.
But the truth is, we love it,
 we really do.

We are in the middle of this season of wonder,
 this time of anticipation that is the Advent of your Son —
and anticipation is truly a wonderful feeling,
 for the realities in our lives, Lord,
 are often unfulfilling and disappointing.

Help us for the moment to forget the cares,
 the shopping, and the gift list;
for right now, we've gathered in this Advent season
 in anticipation.
We're waiting for something good
 that will come into our lives.
We're waiting for the gift you will bring to us,
knowing that it will be the best,
 given in love, given freely.
(continued)

And it will be...
        just what we need.

For that gift, the coming of the Child King,
we give you thanks.
In his name we worship,
        and in his name we give you praise,
    for you are our God of Advent,
        and you do not disappoint.
Amen.

OUR GOD OF ADVENT,
as we retell the Christmas story
    and wait for the celebration of Christmas Day,
    we marvel again that you would send the babe
        to live here, on this planet.
For we learn early in life that it is painful to live here
        on this planet of uncertainty;
    it can be hard here, Lord, and lonely, and meaningless;
    for our spirits often grow cold,
        our hearts lose hope too easily.
And it is painful, sometimes, even to love too much
    or to care too deeply.
So we wait anxiously
    for the birth of the Promised One
    who turns the darkness to light,
    removes the dreaded sting of death,
        and in his birth brings eternal hope.
Our God, we confess now, as your corporate church,
    that we often have been the cause of *your* pain,
and so in the words of our Jewish brethren we pray:
    For the sins which we have committed against you
        under stress or through choice,
        in stubbornness or in error,
        in the evil meditations of the heart,
            by word of mouth,
            by abuse of power,
            by exploiting and dealing treacherously
                with our neighbor,
        bear with us, pardon us, forgive us!
For this we pray in the name of the "Child of Royal Birth,"
    the Savior born unto us
        in the city of David:
            Jesus Christ, the Lord.
    Amen.

Our heavenly Father,
while shepherds watched their flocks
   on that long ago night,
     we were waiting like sheep without a shepherd
     ...lost and without purpose.
We are the flock for whom you've come.
You are the *Great* Shepherd come to save
   and lead and heal us.

It was appropriate that you would choose
   those humble ones
   to be the first to hear the good news
   of the birth of the *Great* Shepherd.
And it is so like you that you would give *them*
the gift of a celestial light show
   they would remember all their lives.
In the day-to-day drudgery of a pastoral life,
they would forever remember that one single moment
   when the heavens opened up
     and angels sang with voices of light.

Our Lord,
often we too yearn for your coming into *our* lives
   with fanfare and joyful noise.
Help us remember that you come humbly
   and gently in our lives
and that it is *we* who should shout and sing;
   it is *we* who are to proclaim the Good News
     of the coming of your Son.
Amen.

CHRISTMAS

Christmas Eve

OUR GOD,
we say good-bye to Advent,
    the hopeful season that brought us to today
    through patient waiting and hopeful expectation.
And we are not disappointed;
it is the magical Christmas Eve.
Today we know that the Lord will come.
Tonight we light the candles of hope
    and partake of the food of the new covenant,
    and in the morning we shall see God's glory,
        the Word made flesh,
        dwelling among us,
        living within us —
        brighter than the flaming sword
        that once cast us from you,
        our eternal and loving God.
This time,
we make room in our hearts and homes
for your coming.
And so we pray,
    Come, Lord Jesus, abide with us.
Amen.

O UR FATHER OF ALL SOULS,
this is Christmas Eve!
There is not another day like this in all the year.
It's as if we have been climbing for the last month
    with our eyes on this one day.
Now we are here — a little spent by our journey —
    but we will enjoy this Christmas Day
        to the fullest!

Our God of Advent,
you have bent low from your heights of holiness
    and looked mercifully upon us,
who, dwelling amid the insecurities of this mortal life,
    are tempted to guard every advantage
    and keep everything
    as if our lives could be secured
        by what we have or can possess.

But you have shown us *your* way,
    your confusing and opposite way of life,
in the giving up of the most precious gift of your Son;
dethroned, uncrowned, powerless, and dependent
    he was given to us.
And we confess that in the end
    we did not know how to receive such a gift —
for we seem to be able to see only gay wrappings
    and bright ribbons that catch our attention —
    and too often miss the *real* gifts in our lives.

But, O God,
what a gift you've given!
In his coming our eyes were opened to how much

we have given ourselves to shadows of unreality,
to killing time and empty distractions.

Now there is light again in our lives!
And our days are filled with meaning,
   for now we know who we are:
children of the King of kings, the Lord of lords,
   the Everlasting Father, the Prince of Peace.
Amen.

OUR MIGHTY GOD,
 who fills the cosmos
 yet was contained in a manger,
 and who today lives in our hearts,
this is the day that was promised to Zion,
 to fear no more,
 for you, our Wonderful Counselor,
  are in our midst,
 the One who gives victory,
 who rejoices over us with gladness,
 who renews us in love,
 and who exults over us in angelic songs
  of goodwill toward all who believe
  the message of this festival day.

So come and visit us in peace,
 find favor in us,
 Our Lord Emmanuel,
 and we will rejoice with renewed hearts.
May our voices of praise
 join with those of the Christmas angels
 as we worship you, our Prince of Peace.
Amen.

Christmastide

OUR GOD OF CELEBRATION,
Christmas Day has come and gone,
and we bask in the afterglow of good feelings
    and new memories fresh from the making.
The gift giving was fun: looking for that one special gift
    that would bring delight to those
        important in our lives.
And the gift getting was nice too, Lord.
For it meant that someone was thinking about *us*.
It meant that we were significant enough in someone's life,
    that they thought about *us*
        and gave a gift of themselves.

And that's what we think on today,
    on the day *after* Christmas.
We think on the mystery that you,
our most holy Creator God,
    would think about *us* and give the gift of yourself.
    And we are left wondering,
        "How do we thank you for such a gift?"

In this Christmastide,
we celebrate the gift of the birth of the Savior,
    born of a virgin in a humble stable,
    announced by both lowly shepherds
        and heavenly angels,
    worshiped by royalty from distant lands,
        and adored by those called by his name.

May his reign on earth continue in our hearts.
    And may our worship today
    be a gift worthy of his majesty.
Amen.

EPIPHANY

Our God of Epiphany; our God of enlightenment;
in this our time of corporate confession,
 we take stock of our living out this week
and hold what we see up to the pure light of your truth.

Here, removed from the dark corners
 where self-deceptions breed,
here, in the presence of your saints
 who hold us to an accounting,
 we see again the shortcomings in our lives;
 for at times we have allowed the baser motivations
 to rule our hearts,
and we have on occasion given in to the easier decisions,
 based on convenience or gain
 rather than grace and integrity.

Forgive us, our God,
 for having turned from your light
 to settle for a cold and colorless world
 of winter gray.
But we have confessed these things,
 and you have shown us mercy.
For like a parent who weighs the anger of the moment
 with the ache of a heart full of love,
 you wash the grime from our guilty faces
 and restore us with a smothering embrace.
And once again we are whole and clean,
 and our eyes are opened to see the colors of life again
 . . . and once again, we know *whose* we are.

Restore to us the joy of your salvation,
that our worship may be pleasing to you today.
Amen.

Advent, Christmas, and Epiphany Prayers

OUR GOD OF LIGHT,
as we continue into this season of Epiphany,
as winter's days grow longer and colder,
the light of the Christmas star fades in our memory
    and the warm feelings of the holidays
        are all but gone.

But the light of that faded star
    is replaced with a greater light:
    the light of your Son, the Light of the World.
In that light we confess our shortcomings,
    knowing that you see all things
        and know our hearts.
Our God, we confess that our hearts have been hard
    and slow to compassion,
    our eyes have been blind to beauty
        and averted from suffering,
    our ears have refused to hear the truth,
        and our lips have been silent
            when injustice claimed her victims,
                even at our doorstep.

These things we confess,
    wishing, truly, to be your children of the Light.
And in the confessing,
    we have your promise of forgiveness.
And in your forgiveness,
    we once again walk in the light of your love.
Amen.

OUR GOD OF THE AGES,
we have brought in a new year
    with celebration and much noise.
We rejoice in the gift of another year of life,
    filled with accomplishments, goals achieved,
    and events that will serve
        as markers for our memory.
    Some of these we will revisit gladly,
        with a distant gleam of joy in our eyes;
    others will invite familiar feelings
        of heartache and loss.

But now it is time for new beginnings,
to welcome second chances and to start again.
We stand on new ground, full of new tomorrows,
    embracing your gift of hope:
    knowing that in your grace
        things do work out,
        bodies do heal,
        relationships mend,
        and life goes on
            in all its mystery and wonder
            and splendor.

Our Lord,
we observe today *your* marker of the new beginning;
we celebrate your sign of the new covenant
    in these simple elements of bread and wine.
May these be a mark for us today
    of the renewing of your covenant in our hearts
    as we remember the gift of new life in Jesus.
Amen.

OUR CREATOR GOD,
you who have set the stars in motion
   and ordered the designs
      and rhythms of our lives,
we join with your creation in her cry of worship of you.
The running brook babbles
   with the joy of your creation;
the stoic mountains rumble and thunder
   but can only hint of your infinite power;
the whispering wind is constant as your presence;
and the hush of the new-fallen snow
   reminds us of the newness of life
   found in your gift of grace
      that makes us new and clean and whole.

And we, with our voices and hearts,
join with the chorus of the creation today,
   and confess that you are our Creator God,
   giver of life abundant
   and alone worthy of our worship.

May our cry of adoration be pleasing to you today.
Amen.

OUR GREAT AND STEADFAST GOD,
you have stayed with us throughout the year,
faithful to your promises, constant in your care,
    and unwavering in your justice.

We stand in your presence, joined in spirit,
    to confess that you are our God,
in whose love we have life
    and in whose light we walk without fear.

Our God of life,
we've grown tired and are no longer amused
    by the gifts of this past Christmas,
    so soon forgotten, it seems.
Yet *your* gift of the new year is novel
    and full, still, of exciting promises,
    like a gift unwrapped.
We pause to confess that at times
    we wasted the coin of the year just past
    and ask your forgiveness, our God,
for all that we ought to have thought
    and have not thought,
all that we ought to have said
    and have not said,
all that we ought to have done
    and have not done.
For thoughts, words, and works ill spent,
    we pray, O God, for forgiveness.

As we plan and scheme how we will parcel out this new year,
    seeking to balance work and play,
    study and leisure,

career and family,
time and money,
and cautiously mindful
    that the year is ours to spend,
    but spend only once,
we pray to be reminded
    that it is glory enough for us
        to be your servants,
    that it is grace enough for us, your church,
        that you should be our Lord.
Amen.

(Adapted from ancient Arabic and Persian prayers)

OUR ETERNAL GOD,
you who are the God of ages past
    and will be our God till the end of time,
we marvel at the familiar stories of our faith;
we delight in accounts of angels hiding in burning bushes
and in stories of kings of ancient worlds in faraway places
and in reading of awesome epiphanies that cause
    patriarchs and spiritual giants to hide their faces.

But, truth be told, our God,
promises of fabled lands flowing with milk and honey
    seem to be as relevant to us as children's fairy tales.
And we confess that often
    we regard the content of our faith
    with no more weight than a child's bedtime story.
The miraculous seems such a thing of the past,
and we do not ask for signs anymore,
    for they are not ours to have, it seems.

In this, our God,
we feel the loss in the insecurity of our faith.
For we *desire* burning bushes
    and voices from heaven
        that knock us off our complacent feet
    with the frightening assurance
        that we are on *holy* ground.
So remind us, our God,
that epiphanies come in many forms;
    in quiet nights and busy days,
    in the company of friend and stranger,
    in the simple living of our complex lives,
and that you who walked with us in the past
will walk with us still.
Amen.

OUR GOD,
our help through all generations,
we are not long into the new year
    and already we've read the lists
    of what's in and what's out.
Where do we learn security in a world of fads,
in a world where the colors on the globes
    in our children's schools
    are outdated before they can master
    the names of most nations and peoples?
For we live in a world that blows hot and cold,
    where change is the only constant
    and the gods of fate play in the fields
        of our careful plans, schemes,
        and hope-filled dreams.

And yet you require of us faith.
Can it be that our only security is to believe?
Can it be that the only true bedrock
    is to be found in a name
    invoked through faith
    when we've cast confidence in all else
    to the wind?

So it is that in that name we pray,
in the One in whom we live and breathe
    and find our meaning,
    Jesus Christ,
    who has been our help in all generations.
Amen.

NEW YEAR'S

An Epiphany New Year's Prayer

OUR GOD OF THE PASSING YEARS,
we count the years and mark our history
    from the quiet beginnings of the humble birth
    of the Christ Child,
    grown in manhood to be our Lord.
And in doing so, we confess that he is the touchstone
    of the beginnings and endings in our lives.
Thank you for all the promises this new year holds in him.
Bless now those who in the coming year
    will serve us with glad hearts,
    those who will share our burdens and laughter,
    those who will challenge us
      to strive for the better way.
Bless those who in the coming year
    will pray for us and ours out of genuine love,
    those who will goad us
      to run the race with integrity,
    those who will inspire us
      with the example of their lives,
    and those who will remember the best we will be
      and who, like true friends, will forget and forgive
      our weaker moments.
Bless now those who in the coming year
      will feed our spirits with song and laughter,
      will heal our bodies with the physician's touch,
      will enlighten us with wisdom and knowledge,
    and these who have come with warm hearts
      on this cold winter night
        to share the joy of Christ.
Amen.

End of Year Prayer

OUR GOD OF AGES,
"It's been a year," as they say —
one filled with accomplishments,
goals achieved, significant birthdays,
and life events that will serve as
    markers for our memories.
Some of these we will revisit gladly
    during times of gathering
        with a distant gleam of joy in our eyes;
and other unbidden moments in our lives' tapestries
    will invite familiar feelings
        of heartache and loss.

Now we replace the calendar on the kitchen wall
and refill our daily planners with fresh pages,
    and it is a time for new beginnings,
    a time for second chances and for starting again.
We have a new year full of tomorrows,
and we embrace your gift of hope,
knowing that in your grace
    things do work out,
    bodies do heal,
    relationships mend,
    and life goes on
        in all its mystery and wonder and splendor.

For the gift of life
and for all the good things you send us
to fill it with meaning and joy,
we give you thanks.
Amen.

Part Two

LENT AND EASTER
PRAYERS

L ENT IS THE PENITENTIAL SEASON of preparation that culminates in the glorious Easter festival. This cycle begins with Ash Wednesday and covers the six Sundays before Easter Day. The forty days of Lent do not include Sundays, which traditionally are considered mini-feast days. The fifth Sunday in Lent is Passion Sunday, followed by Palm Sunday.

Palm Sunday ushers in Holy Week, during which the events of the last week of Jesus' life, his Passion, are the central theme of worship. The Passion culminates on Good Friday, and Easter Sunday celebrates Jesus' glorious resurrection. The forty days of the Easter season conclude with Ascension Day, which commemorates Jesus' exaltation to the right hand of God and affirms his rightful title as King of kings.

LENT

Our God, we begin our Lenten journey
  with excited anticipation,
for it holds the promise of novelty
  and a change from the routine.
But we forget that the roads that will carry us
  on the Lenten journey are rough and unpaved.
In our excitement to get on with the journey,
we forget that the Lenten road is the pilgrim path;
  it is the hard road that bruises,
  it is the unyielding road that trips,
  the uneven road that will force us
      to take our eyes off our destination
      and look instead at our stumbling feet.
But in walking again this purple and crimson path,
  we hope to *see* things — things we've not seen before,
to grasp deeper truths that in earlier stages of life
  have escaped us,
to hear beyond familiar sounding *words*
  to find new meaning for today,
to seek, and in so doing, suddenly to find
  a ray of light in the darkness
  or an insight into the self
  or, at last, coming to the end of our journey,
      to unearth that pearl of great price
      for which we would give...everything.
Our God, be with us on this Lenten journey, we pray,
  for we are ill-equipped to endure
  and too naive to survive the dangers to the spirit.
Walk with us, sustain us,
  for we pray in the name of him
      who has walked this path before us,
          Jesus Christ, the crucified.
Amen.

OUR GOD IN HEAVEN,
we join our hearts with your creation today
in praise of your lordship.

During this Lenten season, we remember when
the creation watched in disbelief
the humbling of the Son of Light
as he stepped from the heavens
    to walk the sod of this earth,
    to share in our hunger and limitations,
    to know the cold and experience the darkness,
    to go unheralded and unrecognized
      as the Creator and Lord,
    and to face the last Enemy
    who steals God's most precious gift of life.

In watchful waiting we re-create that wilderness experience,
confessing that we have not arrived in our personal journeys,
    that we have chosen smoother paths to walk,
    that we have yet a long Lenten journey ahead of us.

But our peace comes in the knowledge that you meet us halfway.
Our comfort is that we do not walk alone, for you have provided
    companions and lovers and friends for the journey.
Our joy is that you also come to us,
    restoring light in darkness,
    hope in the face of death,
    strength in our failings,
    and joy for the living of each day.

And so now with the psalmist we can say,
    Praise the Lord, heaven and earth,
    young and old together: Praise the Lord!
Amen.

OUR LOVING CREATOR, we have gathered today
from our varied stations and scattered places,
   drawn by the light of your wondrous love.

We are mindful today of this strange season
   during which we force ourselves
   to confront the darkness in our lives,
to acknowledge that evil wins its battles too easily in our day,
that pain is real and visits too frequently the innocent,
that death and loss are now familiar friends,
   unbidden and unwelcome,
   but no strangers to our homes.

As your gathered church,
we confess that we have often fallen short
   of being the children of the Light.
For we have allowed the unjust to have their way
   without a word of protest from us;
   we have joined with the oppressors in our silence,
   and we have robbed those in need
      by refusing to be moved to compassion.
Our God, we have your promise, that in confessing these things,
   you are just and faithful in forgiving our shortcomings
   and restoring to us the joy of our salvation.

And so we celebrate this Lenten season,
   not by tarrying on the journey
   nor acknowledging defeat,
   but in keeping our eyes on the Light of your love,
by drawing closer to the ray of hope
   that leaves no shadow on its path
   for its source is your Son,
      the Light that has overcome the world.
Amen.

Our God of covenant,
there may be some today who would ask
   why we gather in this place
   on this spring day to light candles
      against the darkness
   and sing sad songs of crucifixion,
      of mourning and death.
They do not understand that for those called by your name
   the darkness leads to light
   and death yields life
   as surely as the journey through Lent leads to Easter.

Help us proclaim your message of love
that they may know that when we gather to worship
we merely confess that you are God,
   that you are our God,
   the faithful One, who loves us
   and has called us
   and has brought us to this day
   and who alone is worthy of our worship.
Amen.

O<small>UR</small> G<small>OD</small>,
it is to our shame that we make the confession
    that, like straying sheep who have turned a deaf ear
    to the guiding voice of the shepherd,
    we *too easily* tend to stray from the Lenten path
    and lose our way in wildernesses
    of our own making.
But at least give us credit, Lord,
for confessing our shame —
that is not a virtue we teach today.
Our nation's leaders seem not to model it often;
    we hardly recognize it in ourselves,
    and our children may not come to learn it.
But we gather to worship today
the One who in his infinite love
    was able to bear our shame and make it his,
who took it out of our reach beyond death
    and made us whole.
For the gift of new life in Christ,
    for the death that sealed it,
    for the love that gave it,
    and for the hope that confirms it,
        may your name be praised, our God.
Amen.

OUR GREAT SHEPHERD,
you feed our spirits,
   search for us when we are lost,
   bind our injuries,
   and strengthen us when we are weak.
We *know* about Lenten journeys, our God,
   for we have walked them,
and some among us, even now, are on the Lenten journey
   through weary paths of uncertainty
     that blind us to hope,
   through dry spiritual deserts
     that leave us parched and thirsty for rest.

But you have taught us, in faith,
   to press on through the rocky paths
   that cause our feet to slip and our hearts to stumble;
for you are the Shepherd who rescues us
   from days of clouds and darkness
     to bring us to the green pastures of springtime.

Walk with us this journey, our Shepherd,
and that will be sufficient.
For in our hearts we know that this purple path of denial
leads to a crimson-stained cross of hope,
   and we know the triumphant One
   who walked this way before us.
Amen.

OUR GOD,
who calls us to this Lenten journey,
we confess that we falter at walking this path
   to which we've set our feet,
      lacking the singleness of purpose
         that compelled you to walk it.

We confess that we often fail to take
   the deliberate next step
   that will carry us
   closer to our destination.
For we are uncomfortable with the attire
   of solitude and self-denial,
   sacrifice and simplicity
   that we need for this journey.
We are too easily distracted
   by the barkers on the side of the road
      who draw our attention
      to more appealing attractions;
   we eagerly allow the tyranny of activity
      and business as usual
      to engage us in small talk
         even as other Lenten pilgrims pass us by.

So help us, we pray,
   to continue again our journey,
   to walk with those around us
   who carry burdens of doubt and uncertainty,
   who limp along the Lenten path
      in their woundedness,
   who would sit in the middle of the road
   and just give up
   (continued)

because they are weary
from lack of hope.
Call us again to the journey
for their sake
and for our own.
For only at the end of the path to the cross
will we find again
the hope that sustains us,
the grace that saves us,
and the love that leads to life
and life abundant.

In the name of your Son, Jesus Christ,
who walks before us.
Amen.

OUR GOD,
immortal, invisible Creator,
we enter this Lenten season
   with the hope of spring in our midst.
The bleakness of winter has given way
   to warm sunshine.
We've dared to cast off our heavy coats
   and have spied children on bicycles and skateboards
   reclaiming the sidewalks from the once frozen snow.

We are grateful for the reminders of hope,
for we intend in this Lenten time
   to respect the harsher realities of our faith:
   that hope follows despair,
   that forgiveness requires repentance,
   that hurt precedes healing,
   and that life flows out of death.

And so we confess, our God,
our reluctance to walk the Lenten journeys,
   to engage in the honest disciplines
   of prayer, confession, and repentance,
      for who can argue with you?

Guide us through the pilgrim's path, we pray,
   that we may find fellowship with your Son
   and with those who choose to walk with us
   this forty days' journey to hope.
Amen.

OUR GOD, who dwells in the heavens
but is here among us and in us and with us,
you have called us in this season to walk
    the Lenten journey,
  a gray path of repentance, sacrifice, and denial,
  on which we turn to face death,
  standing in the distance,
  waiting at the end of our bleak journey,
    eager to shock us in its embrace
  as we allow the full realization of its certainty
    to chill our spines and hollow our hearts
    and numb our souls
  as we marvel at its power to kill
    even the Son of God.

But we confess today, our God,
that it has been difficult
    to practice gloomy spiritual disciplines this week,
    simply because spring is finally here.
Around the base of spindly trunks
    of seemingly lifeless trees and shrubs,
  poking up through the mulch of dead bark
  and dry brittle leaves,
  new life, new hope bud upward toward the sun,
    as daffodils and crocuses.

In the gray Lenten season, we are distracted
  by this yellow and purple life
  blooming in the midst of windy chill
  and in the aftermath of winterdeath,
  reminding us that death was conquered
    on the other side of the Lenten journey,

when death embraced the Son of God
and was smothered by God's love.

Thank you, God, for your gift of hope,
    so colorful and certain,
    for reminding us that
    though the Lenten journey
    must be completed,
    there is hope at its end
        in new life in your Son, Jesus Christ.
Amen.

PALM SUNDAY

Our God and Savior,
who alone is worthy of all glory and honor,
we near the end of our Lenten journey
   on this Palm Sunday
filled with both anticipation and aversion,
for to end this journey
   is to ascend the hill of ultimate sacrifice.

We receive you today as your triumphant church,
   singing hosannas,
for you have ascended the hill of God
   and have stood in God's holy place
   with clean hands and a pure heart,
and in so doing have secured our status
   as daughters and sons of God.

We confess, our God,
that too often we have been content
to be spectators on the side of the road
   willing to receive you and honor you
   but reluctant to follow,
   timid in finishing the journey.
We readily accept the gift of life eternal,
   which is given freely,
   but comes only on the other side of the shadowed cross.

And so we pray,
ride into our lives once again;
give us the faith to finish our journey of faith,
not as spectators but as followers
   faithful to the end of our days.
Amen.

EASTER

Our God of Resurrection,
our long Lenten journey,
begun in the bleak of winter
and now finished in the springtime
   with its budding signs of hope,
has brought us through the night
   to the foot of the cross
      and now to an empty tomb.

We thank you for this Easter day,
for the miracle of the resurrection of our rightful King,
   who has washed our sins away
   and conquered death
   and given us the gift of life.

We praise you for this Easter Day,
for today the great adventure begins:
   new life, true life,
   free from the sin that would enslave us,
   free from the fear of death that would claim us,
   free to love fully and completely,
   as you have loved us.

May your name be praised.
Amen.

OUR GOD IN HEAVEN,
on this high holy day,
when all believers gather in celebration
  of the ultimate hope
  realized through that once-obscure wandering teacher
  who hid his identity well in humility and meekness,
we confess our shortcoming —
  our failure to live out that resurrection reality in our lives —
    our inability to die to sin completely.
We confess our lack of faith,
  which keeps us huddled near the empty tomb,
    peering into the hollow darkness of doubt
    while the world behind us is blooming with new life,
    pushing itself out of the cold earth
    into the warmth of resurrected living.
Make real in us today, our God, we pray,
  the mystery of the wonder of our resurrected Christ.
May the power of that first Easter morning,
  witnessed by few, believed by many,
    that morning when death lost its sting,
    when fear lost its claim on our hearts,
    when despair was banished
    and hope rose resplendent like the morning sun,
  May that power be real in our hearts today.
Hallelujah! Christ is risen.
  So may your name be praised.
Amen.

OUR GOD OF LIFE,
the earth blooms today in celebration
    of its memory of the resurrection of our Lord.
In the rainbow tulips, in the delicate daffodils and tender buds,
we see that the earth remembers the morning after,
    when darkness was replaced by a dawn
    unlike any other seen before,
when despair was replaced by unbridled joy,
    defeat by ultimate victory,
    and death was shredded by the shards from the blast
        of a sealed stone that couldn't contain
            the power of your love.

And so, we your church
can gather at this river by the waters of baptism
    to celebrate your perpetual gift of new life to us.
After the despair of the cross,
    that spectacle of the worst that lives within us —
        our cowardliness, our apathy,
        our betrayal of your love, our sin,
        and the unyielding, unrelenting certainty of mortal death —
you remove the rock that encloses our tombs of doubt,
    you remove the sting of death,
    and in the light of your love
    we come to know that your Son is the true
        Lamb of God
        who takes away the sin of the world.

And so we confess: "Worthy is the Lamb who was slain."
Praise and honor, glory and might,
    to the God who sits on the throne,
        and to the Lamb forever.
May your name be praised.
Amen.

EASTERTIDE

Our everlasting God,
the world rejoices this Eastertide
  with signs of resurrection.
Trees are budding
  and bulbs are surrendering their secret colors
    kept hidden throughout the winter
    buried under dirt and snow;
and the sound of nesting birds
and of the occasional lawn mower
  tells us that the long winter
  may indeed be over at last.

These are welcome signs of hope,
  for despite the reality of the resurrection of our Lord
our world at times, we confess, seems deaf to the cry of hope
  from the empty tomb.
Good men still die.
Our prisons are full.
Faithful women still cry for lost husbands and children
  in war-torn countries.
And children starve for lack of food and love,
  still.

Give hope to such as these we pray, our God.
And for ourselves we pray
  that you would make hope our constant companion.
For we know that your hope is the cord strong enough
  to hold life together
  when all else unravels around us,
  and without it, even dreams may perish.
Amen.

Lent and Easter Prayers

Part Three

PRAYERS FOR
THE COMMON TIME

T HE SEASON OF THE COMMON TIME begins with the feast of Pentecost (also called Whitsunday) fifty days after the Passover. This is the longest season of the Christian Year, and it concerns itself with the ministry of the Holy Spirit in the life of the church.

In the early church the day of Pentecost was observed by feasting and became a favorite occasion for baptizing converts into the family of faith. Pentecost is the third great Christian feast after Christmas and Easter.

The first Sunday after Pentecost is Trinity Sunday. This is the only Sunday in the Christian year given to a particular doctrine of the church, highlighting the centrality of this confessional belief of the Christian church.

GOD

OUR HEAVENLY FATHER,
you have called us your children, and such we are.
As our heavenly Parent,
   in your power you have given us life,
   in your wisdom you have called us each by name,
   in your love you have given us the freedom
   to walk our own paths,
   and in your grace, you have redeemed us.

We have gathered today as children returning to a homecoming,
   seeking direction in the lives we've made for ourselves,
   seeking comfort for our sorrows,
   seeking identity in a world seemingly gone mad,
   seeking the wisdom to make right and nobler choices,
   seeking to find the home where we belong —
   but more, gathering to celebrate the source
      of our life and living.

In our gathering, we confess that
   no matter how grown-up we've become,
   you remain Daddy and Mommy,
that no matter how competent we've grown,
   we will always need you,
that no matter how successful we've been,
   we will always seek your approval.

Give us today the blessing that will confirm
   that we are your children.
Father, as we gather here today,
   may your children's voices of praise
   be pleasing to you.
Amen.

Oᴜʀ ʟɪᴠɪɴɢ Gᴏᴅ,
you who are not made with human hands
   nor conceived in finite minds,
we remember today the lessons of Sunday school,
   lessons of an *awesome* God,
      whose arms can span the universe,
      whose fingertips can touch the edges of the cosmos
         (without stretching!),
      who watches "from up above, looking down with love."
Remind us, O God, to be careful . . .
   our little eyes of what we see,
   our little ears, what we hear,
   our little feet, where we walk.

We confess today our predilection for smaller gods,
   those more manageable than you,
      less awesome, more tame,
      ones who know the value of . . . negotiations,
      and who respect our space,
   polite gods, who wait to be asked
      and who tolerate our will for ourselves
      and the designs and schemes we lay down for our lives.

Deliver us today, we pray,
   from gods and idols made by our own hands,
for though our craft may delight our eyes,
   and our power, which shapes and scars our world,
      indeed is awesome,
our hearts have not yet grown fully
   into the image of your Son, Jesus Christ.
So lest we deceive ourselves and lose our center, call us back,
   that we may have no other gods before you.
May our worship today be pleasing to you, the living God.
Amen.

OUR GOD,
you who alone are holy and worthy of our praise,
we your church come in confession and in need,
for we are a people of unclean lips and stubborn hearts,
    who have yet to learn how to live
    beyond our halfhearted, half-loving ways.

Finish the work you began in us, we pray.
Through your Spirit make our meek hearts bold
    that we may serve you boldly,
make our fisted hands open
    that we may serve others freely,
and make our spirits free
    that we may move and breathe in the gentle winds
        of the Spirit,
    who guides and prompts,
    who burns and cleanses.

And having confessed, we are forgiven,
and having asked, we have received,
    for such is your promise.
    And your promises are as sure
    as the bedrock of our faith:
    Jesus Christ, the Savior.

May your name be praised.
Amen.

O<small>UR</small> G<small>OD</small>,
you for whom the mountains bow low
and the valleys level to meet your majestic stride,
in the living of these days,
    uncertainty is our constant reality.
We have come to accept that much of our life
    is lived in the dust of the mundane,
and we seek to measure our lives by the moments
    of gentler remembrances.

Mountaintop experiences are rare for us, our God;
    sometimes strings of trivial activities
    seem to be the only things
        that tie our days together.
So we marvel that you would leave your splendor
    to trudge atop the dust of this planet,
    to tire, to hunger, to hurt,
        as we do.

But that is good news,
for now we pray with confidence
to a God who knows the rhythm of our lives
    and joins us in the cycles of laughter and tears,
    in seasons of celebration and grief.
For your constancy in our lives, our God,
    for your pursuing love and redeeming grace
    in our Savior Jesus Christ,
        we are grateful.
Amen.

THE CHURCH

O<small>UR</small> C<small>REATOR</small> G<small>OD</small>,
you to whom we turn to give meaning
  to work and vocation,
in our day of limited resources,
  of corporate downsizing and rightsizing,
  of tight budgets and nervous deficits,
  the words of your ancient prophet
    are a welcome relief.

We breathe a sigh of relief to know
you do not require of us
  modern-day equivalents of burnt offerings;
  you do not ask for costly gifts
    or 20 percent off the top.
And you say you are not impressed
  by bulk-sized offerings,
  for when it comes down to worshiping you,
    you say our money is no good here.

But our sense of relief is short-lived,
  for what you do ask of us is hard:
    "to do justice,
    to love kindness,
    and to walk humbly."
And we come to realize it would be easier
  to give our money than to care,
  to pay the tithe than to fight injustice,
  and to fulfill our obligations than to walk humbly.

But we understand.
What you most want of us,
(continued)

what you need,
what would be your heart's desire,
   is that we give our selves,
      not what we have
      or can afford to give up
      or can do without.
You want *us*, whom you've called your people,
   your church.

Grant to us today, through your Spirit,
   the capacity to worship you
   in Spirit and truth,
      that our worship may be pleasing to you.
Amen.

OUR CREATOR GOD,
you who birthed your church
    with rushing wind and tongues of fire,
in this season of Pentecost
we celebrate the life of your church.
You have redeemed us and called us the bride of Christ,
    and so we have become a new creation,
called to live in faith and action,
    to light the world with your love,
    and to toil to realize your kingdom on earth
        as it is in heaven.

But we would confess, our God,
    that often we have lived in the shadow of the old nature,
    living in the illusion of the security of the certain
        rather than in faith.
And we have hidden our light from the eyes of the world
    by keeping it behind the vanity of amenability
    and the opaque curtain of accommodation.

And yet in our blindness we weep
that the kingdoms of this earth
    are not as in your heaven.
You have promised, O God,
that you will forgive our weaknesses
    if we confess them in the name of your Son,
        and so we trust in your word
        and celebrate the liberating truth
that the expanse of oceans and cultures
    do not separate your church,
        just as the expanse between heaven and earth
        cannot separate us from your redeeming love.
Amen.

OUR GOD OF GRACE,
what a mystery is your church.
You have called us your bride despite our unfaithfulness;
you have entrusted the hope of the world
        to our fickle compassion.

You have chosen to relieve the hunger, pain, and suffering
    of our world, not by a wave of a wand,
    but by giving us
        arms to build and embrace,
        hands to teach and heal,
        voices to fight injustice,
    beautiful feet to bring Good News,
and hearts to redeem in the power of your love.

Our God of glory,
what a wonder is your church:
    a community of sinners learning to be saints,
    an army of wounded healers,
    scarred, often battered,
    still persecuted,
        yet triumphant!

We, your church, have gathered to confess today
    that you are our God —
    Creator, Redeemer, and King,
    now and forever.
May our worship today be worthy of you.
Amen.

OUR HEAVENLY GOD, you who are Spirit and Truth,
once again we have gathered as your people
   to give your church a face
   and hands and a voice.
Open our eyes to see your face,
   and then we will see the faces
      of our sisters and brothers,
the smooth faces of innocent babes,
   and the nobly wizened faces of our elders —
for to see your face is to recognize the face
   of the one we call stranger,
      but whom you call your own.

Open our eyes to see your hands,
and then we will see the hands
   of those who touch our lives in the flesh,
the physician who heals, the lover who comforts,
   and the friend who tells us we belong here.
Lord, there are hands in our lives we do not see:
   those who care for us in uncelebrated ways —
   hands lifted in prayer for us,
   hands that cook and wash
   and clean and build for us,
   hands that work
   and then share the fruits of their labor
      with pride and gratitude.

Open our ears to hear your voice,
   and we will hear the truth that will set us free.
We may hear it in the voices of our children,
   who are not ashamed to ask honest questions
   (continued)

or to point out the emperor's new clothes
when we would be too polite to admit our discomfort.

As the wind moves the trees
and scatters the fall leaves across our yard,
so may the voice of your Spirit move our spirits
and blow away from our eyes the dust of illusions
that makes the world look gray.
May its breeze fill our lungs with new life,
fresh and cool as this November morning.
May your Spirit reveal your liberating truth to us today,
and when we are able to see these things, our God,
we will have cause to praise you,
for you have given us good things to fill our lives,
and you have given your truth to set us free.
Amen.

OUR GREAT SHEPHERD,
whose voice we know,
who leads us to still waters
and restores our souls through the Spirit of love,
we have no words to thank you for your gentle care.

You have kept us for this day to be your church in this world,
to be a part of it, not apart from it,
to run toward it in love, not from it in fear.

Our God,
do not allow us to sit with folded hands
while a neighbor in the city goes hungry.
Do not let us keep silent
while there is a child in need of a word of encouragement.
Do not let us become comfortable
while there are yet lost sheep of your flock in prisons.
And do not let us withhold our hand
while there are places in this world that can feed a family
for the price of a soft drink.

For by your grace we have been empowered
and in your love you have called us
to be your hands of compassion,
your voice of redemption,
and your arms of love
to a hurting and needy world.
Amen.

OUR GOD, you have created us
and in your love have set us free,
  but it's hard to know, sometimes, who to serve.

Like the people of Israel long ago,
  we often imagine greener pastures from a new king
    or a new boss;
  and the truth is, as the man sang,
    "We've all got to serve somebody."

And we confess today that we are prone to seek
    other kings to serve;
  those who seem not to make demands of sacrifice,
  those who seem to let us have our own way,
  those who would give what satisfies
    for the moment of expedience,
      with no concern for what is right or true
        or honest or good.

As we focus our hearts on the worship of you,
  our true and rightful King of heaven,
remind us that our allegiance to you
    has never been out of obligation
    but is a response to your grace,
that our obedience is not out of a sense of debt
    but is a confession of devotion,
that our love for you is not from dependence
    (for you have set us free and given us all things)
      but from the wonder that you should love us
      and would give us the gift of eternal life
        in your Son, Jesus Christ.

May your name be praised.
Amen.

OUR GOD,
giver and sustainer of life,
we know about roads,
the ones not taken,
    the ones that converge in a wood,
    or the ones that, midway upon the journey of life,
    lead us to find ourselves within a dark forest
       when the straight path has been lost.

We confess our discomfort, our God,
with the knowledge that the journey on the road of life
    offers no signposts,
    no mileage markers.
And so we create our own —
    birthdays and anniversaries,
    rites of passage
    and first accomplishments
       (first job, first car, first home,
       first promotion, first child) —
    and we note the dates in our journals
    to assure ourselves
       that we are "getting there."

In our restlessness we continue on the road,
believing that the landscape of life
    will make sense only when the journey is over
       and we can look back.
But in our better moments
we know that in the pilgrimage of the soul
    these are but illusions of movement
    and that in the wonder of your grace,
       in the company of the Savior
       (continued)

who walks with us,
we have arrived.

On this journey of life, our God,
    may we find rest in you.
Give us direction for the journey, we pray,
    and friends for the traveling.
    And for the companionship of the Spirit,
        who leads us in the way we are to walk,
we thank you in the name of Jesus,
our Lord and friend.
Amen.

O<small>UR</small> G<small>OD</small>,
you who are our ever-present help,
it is we, as your church —
    gathered in the name of Jesus the Christ, our Savior —
who call upon you today
    to be with those who in their loneliness
    seek your comforting embrace.
We call upon you today
    to heal those who, being sick in body and spirit,
    long for your physician's touch.
We call upon you today
    to protect the weak, the frightened,
        and the falsely accused,
    who depend now only on *your* power to save.
We call upon you today
    to meet us in life's shadowed valleys of doubts
    and at life's corners where the unexpected winds of change
        blow uncertain on our hearts.

Teach us to look and enable us to see
    that you are to be found in the familiar stuff of life —
    in common places and gentle faces —
    that you come to those
        who in humbleness of spirit
        and in confession of need
        lift their eyes unto the hills
        seeking the Maker of heaven and earth
            who is our ever-present help.
We pray this as your church
    called into being in the name of Jesus our Savior.
Amen.

CONFESSION

Our Father in heaven,
your church has gathered to worship here,
   in this place we have built with care and pride.

In this worship room, we set aside space for a miracle:
we give flesh and bone and faces to your church —
Faces young and old,
   faces we have grown accustomed to seeing
      in their usual places,
   faces we have come to love as brother and sister.
And here there is space for a greater miracle —
   you fill this room with your presence.
You are here!
Among us, around us, within us.

What a miracle to confess
      that the God of the universe,
      the Lord of the heavens,
      is among us.
Our God, we acknowledge that too often
   the miracle is lost on us.
Too often we gather unfocused and unaware
   that you are here,
   in the shape of this room,
   in the lights and the colors,
      and the music and the voices.

But most of all,
you are in the faces of your church —
   these with whom we worship.
Help us now to see your divine presence,

for our world clamors for our attention,
    and we are easily distracted.

We have become used to giving attention
    only to that which is the loudest and the brightest,
    the newest and shiniest distractions
        that vie for our attention.
Help us now to see your divine presence.
Remind us that you often choose to come to us
    in quiet and unobtrusive ways —
in a quiet voice, a whisper, a sighing babe,
and very often, in the faces of those who are your church.
Teach us to find you there.
Amen.

O<small>UR</small> G<small>OD</small>,
we call on you today
as the people called into being through your Spirit,
confident that you are the God who listens to our supplications.

You heard us when we cried for a Savior,
    and you sent your Son.
You heeded our trembling voices when we cried in the darkness,
    and you sent the Light of life and love,
And you hear our prayers in the uncertainty of our lives,
    and you send us the sustaining hope.

Hear now our prayers of confession for our sake;
for we are a people hard of hearing
who do not readily learn your lessons of grace
    that to believe is to obey,
    that to give away is to gain,
    and that to be your child
    is to never be separated from your love;
        for neither death nor life, neither angels nor demons,
        neither height nor depth,
        nor anything *else* in all creation
        will be able to separate us from the love of God
            that is in Christ Jesus our Lord.

For this we worship you
    and will forever call you our God.
May your name be praised.
Amen.

OUR GOD,
we confess that hearing your voice
seems to be more difficult for us these days,
for there is much to distract us
and much to entertain us
    that tickles our ears
    and delights our eyes;
        and we do seek these distractions out,
for it is hard to think constantly
    on the more sober matters of the Spirit.
So teach us to listen for your voice
    over the clatter of daily distractions,
    above the din of our busy activities.
Send us companions of the inner way
    who can teach us to recognize the cries
        of those who need our prayers,
        who seek our attention of love,
        and who need of the overflow of our abundance,
        which comes from you.
Amen.

O<small>UR</small> G<small>OD</small>,
we hear the Spirit of benevolence and grace
you want us to show to the world.
But it is a difficult thing for us,
    we confess,
for our enemies are convenient,
    and our anger is . . . useful.

So help us, we pray,
to accept your lovingkindness
and the forgiveness that comes through your Son,
    so that we, in turn, may
        forgive those who dismiss us,
        love the unlovely,
        pray for the good of those who hurt us,
        and give of ourselves to those who would deny us.

For in this way we honor life
and grow in the Spirit of our Savior,
Jesus Christ.
Amen.

OUR GOD,
in whose presence we come
    seeking solace and communion,
we often wonder, our Creator,
    what have we lost in leaving the Garden?
Our innocence, certainly — once lost,
    that can never be regained;
    and so it is that we hold newborn babies
    close to our bosom,
sweet reminders of a way of being that is ephemeral,
    too quickly lost
        even in children.

We confess today, our God,
    our continued habit of choosing
    less than what you desire for us.
We are capricious children, Lord,
    too easily tempted by forbidden fruit,
    too ready to accept the lure of comfort
        and empty promises,
    quick to forget that all is ours already
    in your grace and love.

Prepare for us again, we pray,
    a place of peace, a place of belonging,
    a place of work in which our souls
    will find a home.
Amen.

OUR GOD OF VISION,
who comes to us in our waking and sleeping,
    who speaks to your people through bold prophets
    and whispers unbidden in the quiet hidden recesses
        of our secret minds,
we gather away from the noisome world
    to seek your presence
        in the company of your people.
We come to seek focus in our lives,
    away from the many voices
        crying for our attention.
And we come in hope that you will once again speak to us
    and help us find the true center of our lives,
        that we may find the guiding visions
            and choose the path of destiny that is your will.

Our God,
we confess that without you
we are lost, and so we pray:
    give dreams to the hopeless
    and vision to the powerless
    and hope to all those who seek you.
Amen.

O<small>UR</small> G<small>OD</small>,
so often we want to believe that our faith
should lead to security;
that to believe in you, our almighty God,
   is to be insulated from the harsher realities of living
   and that to be faithful is always to win.

We confess that these are the myths of our faith.
This is our wishful thinking,
   our insecure prayer that
   thy will be done on earth,
   as it is in heaven.
But, in our more honest moments, Lord,
we know that the truth lies on this side
   of any imagined Nirvana.
It is in the struggles of living
   when your grace is greatest in us.
   Pain is our sign of healing,
   despair leads to hope,
   death births life,
   and in our weakness you manifest your power.

So deliver us, we pray,
   from the slumber of our comfort,
   from our myths of perfection,
   and from our desire for security over passion;
   for certainty over adventure,
   and from the self-sufficiency
   that allows no room for the faith
   that opens the greater possibilities you keep for us
      if we choose to believe.
Amen.

FAITH

Dᴇᴀʀ Gᴏᴅ, when you walked this earth, days were simpler.
A day's journey was measured by footsteps
  rather than by speed limits.
To talk to someone was to be within touching distance,
  to look into the eyes of the other person.
We "talk" through faxes and car phones,
  satellites and cyberspace,
    never really touching, becoming faceless to one another,
    like voices crying in the wilderness.

We envy your simple world, for ours has become complex.
The distractions are many in our time.
Many things compete for our attention,
  and not getting it, they dazzle our eyes
  and raise the volume and tempt our senses.
We have become accustomed to being easily distracted,
and it has become easier to look about us
  rather than to look upward for comfort,
  easier to look around us
    than to look inward for meaning.

Our God,
in our busy, cluttered world, we long to see your face,
  to hear simple words of love and healing,
  to find a quiet place in your arms,
  to be touched by your grace,
  to be heard without yelling.

And so this is our prayer for this hour of worship:
keep our minds on you that we may know your peace,
open our eyes to your love that we may see your beauty,
and quiet our hearts that we may hear your voice.
Amen.

Prayers for the Common Time

OUR HEAVENLY FATHER,
we've set aside space in this room
    for your healing presence.
We've made room in our hearts
    for faith to work,
and we've made room in our minds for wholeness.

When you were with us, walking this earth,
you touched and healed,
and you said that we, your church,
    would do greater works than these.

So we have gathered together as your children,
    in your name,
to do the great work of confessing our needs
    for healing of heart
        and soul and mind.
And in so doing, we begin to do the redemptive work
    of healing the sicknesses and weaknesses
    that befall us as children of the world.

We seek for ourselves, who are your children,
and for those whom you love and we hold dear,
the touch that would heal and bring wholeness of spirit
    and wellness of being.
Amen.

HOPE

Our God of hope,
who has proven your steadfast love for us
throughout the generations,
today we pray for this generation,
for we seem to be living out that ancient Chinese curse
    that would wish for us to live in "interesting times."

And our days are interesting:
    our illusions of a wholesome and safe heartland
    have been shattered
    by visions of devastation
    and the broken bodies of our children.
The symbols of our nation are held in contempt,
    and our political leaders today seek refuge
    not only behind words
    but also behind closed streets and concrete barriers.
And to make a life for oneself today, our God,
    offers no guarantees of security or fulfillment,
    and the toll exacted on our spirits and on our families
        is too often severe.

And so, our God,
we thank you today for that most constant of gifts,
    our hope through our Savior, Jesus Christ.
In him we can hope that the patterns of our lives
    will change always for the better.
In "interesting times," when life unravels
and there seems to be nothing to hold on to,
    your gift of hope is the thread that is strong enough
    to hold life together.
With it, our dreams never perish.
May your name be praised.
Amen.

COMMUNION

Our Great Shepherd,
we observe today that simple ceremony you left us.
With ordinary elements of bread and drink,
   we remember that night in which you,
   the Great Shepherd,
   became the slain Lamb of sacrifice.

Through this familiar ritual in which we find hope,
we remember that night you left the comfort
      of ritual and familiarity
   to enter the chaos of the unknown.

You left the well-lit upper room and the safety of friends
   to enter the darkness that would overcome the Light.
And ultimately you set aside your power
   and laid down your life to give us the gift of eternal life.

Before celebrating the glorious end of that night,
   through partaking of these elements,
   we your church would confess
   that we have at times not loved
      as deeply as we should
      in receiving the stranger among us,
      in honoring the humble,
      in visiting the poor,
      in speaking justice on behalf of the oppressed.

Forgive us, for we confess,
   "Worthy is the Lamb that was slain
      to receive power and riches,
      wisdom and strength,
      honor and glory and praise."
Amen.

OUR GOD IN HEAVEN,
we have gathered around your table today
    in answer to your call to remembrance.
Through our ritual
        we remember your gifts of love,
through our music
        we celebrate your Spirit,
through our words
        we proclaim your triumph,
    and in our gathering together
        we confess your lordship.

And we gather in spirit with others of your church
    who on this day meet
    not in the daylight of spring
    but in the cover of secret, hidden places,
who sing their songs of hope
    in whispered tones
but whose worship from the heart
    rings loud and true
    and reaches your throne.

We join our voices with them in praise of you,
and we join our hearts to theirs
    in a prayer for deliverance.
Amen.

OUR CREATOR GOD,
you who are immortal, invisible, and wise,
once again we gather around this familiar table,
    this table that says so much about us,
    this table with spiritual elements upon which we feed,
        and in so doing, try to remember, as you asked of us.

We try to remember your words,
    spoken in whispers with a haunted voice
        in the knowledge of what was to come that night,
    spoken in love for us and for our sake,
    spoken in confidence that the life you would give up
        would be restored to you, in honor and power.

We try to remember that we come to this table always seeking,
    seeking assurance of your love,
        for we forget too quickly that you love us,
    seeking forgiveness, for we give in too easily,
    seeking the comfort of those around us, who care for us,
    seeking the rhyme and reason that will give meaning
        to our lives
    in this often hectic and confusing world.

And in seeking these things, we are found,
    and in asking, we become able to give,
    because around your table
    we find all these and more
        in your loving presence.
Amen.

O God,
these stories in the Old Testament are sometimes ... strange.
We do not understand casual dialog with the Holy One
  or animal sacrifices
  or smoking firepots with floating blazing torches.

Visions make us uncomfortable,
  and your angry judgments
  are a side of you we'd rather not see.
And those names, Lord, well ...
  they're just hard to pronounce.

But we do understand your promises.
And we do understand that
  unlike our uncertain contracts,
  weak handshakes,
  halfhearted pledges,
  and lip service to even the most sacred of tasks,
  your promises are true.

For the promise to father Abraham,
  fulfilled in our Lord Jesus Christ
  and celebrated at this table
  with our own covenant symbols of blood and flesh,
    wine and bread,
we thank you as we celebrate your continuing promise
  of hope and redemption.
Amen.

OUR GOD, who dwells in the highest
and who has called us to be church
   in your Son, Jesus Christ,
we thank you today
for the rich heritage we claim as Christians,
   a heritage born of courage, piety, and sacrifice.

We claim today
fellowship in mission with all believers,
   as we give of our wealth
   for the work of your church
      around the world
   in healing the sick
   and feeding the hungry,
   in proclaiming your Word
      that the blind may see,
   and in so doing, freeing the captives
      in the name of Jesus of Nazareth.

We claim today
communion with all the saints,
   as we partake of the wine and the bread —
   symbols of blood and body,
   symbols of love incarnate.

We confess, our God,
   that in the comfort of your blessings of abundance
   and in the safety of the blessing of peace in our land,
   we too easily forget those of our body, your church,
   who pray for your daily bread
      to feed their hungry children,
      (continued)

who pray for signs of peace in their land,
who pray for freedom to pursue a life worth the living.

So in approaching your table, make us mindful, we pray,
that others of your church today
eat the bread in secret for fear of persecution
and drink the cup in whispers for fear of death.
For them, our sisters and brothers, we pray
that your Spirit will watch over them
with a mighty arm,
that your joy may be complete in them,
and that their hope in you may be realized in power.

These things we pray in the mighty name
of the One who makes us one,
Jesus Christ, our Savior.
Amen.

OUR GOD,
we celebrate today your calling to your church
    to engage in missions.

It sometimes seems anachronistic to ask people
to give of themselves,
for we've become accustomed
    to the convenience of the checkbook.
It is easier, we confess, to give of our means
    than to give of ourselves.

And so we thank you for your call to us, your church,
that would shake us from our complacency and comfort —
    to make disciples of all people,
    to feed the hungry,
    to visit the prisoner,
    to welcome the stranger,
    to love the unlovely,
    to visit the widow and orphan,
really, to be your hands and feet
    during our time of pilgrimage in this world.

We thank you for all those from among us
who have answered that call to missions
    here in our neighborhood,
    in foreign lands and different cultures here and abroad.
May their faithfulness be our example,
    and may your love for your world
    be our motivation.
Amen.

Oᴜʀ Gᴏᴅ,
the occasional coolness in the night air
and the anticipatory colors on the few impatient trees
hint that a leisurely change of seasons is upon us.
  This summer will soon recede into its slumber,
  and the crisp fall will lead us
  into our next cycle of living and being.

Here we gather yet again
beginning another month,
another cycle of the moon,
another page on the calendar,
  another round of bills to pay,
  meetings to attend, appointments to keep,
  another communion Sunday —
  all markers for the cycles in our lives.

And gathered around this table of fellowship
we again eat and drink of these simple elements
transformed in death through the power of resurrection
into the new covenant of life in Jesus Christ.

Through this act of obedience,
today we again will covenant with you
and with each other to walk with you
  and to love you and to seek you
  in all our seasons and cycles,
  in all our ways and days.

May your name be praised.
Amen.

Oᴜʀ Gᴏᴅ,
we come together as your church —
    once again gathering around this familiar table
    to practice our remembrance of you.

But we confess, our God, that your invitation
    to fellowship at this holy table
        both draws and repels us.
For our yearning to share
    in the love and grace of your table
    moves us *first* to confession:
that we are not worthy
    and so we are grateful for your embracing grace,
that we are a forgetful people
    and so we are grateful for your steadfast love,
that we are prone to embrace our temptations
    and so we pray for *your* strength,
that we are too often proud of what is not to our merit
    and so we pray for humility of spirit,
that we are too quick to judge and too slow to compassion
    and so we pray for your helper Spirit
        to cleanse, convict, and renew.

And having made our confession,
    we hold fast to your promise of wholeness and healing
    and come gladly to share these simple elements
        with these your people,
        your church,
    redeemed in your Son, Jesus Christ,
        our Savior.
Amen.

THANKSGIVING

Oᴜʀ Cʀᴇᴀᴛᴏʀ Gᴏᴅ,
giver of life and provider of all *good* things,
who has blessed us in the gift of new life
   in the Savior, Jesus Christ,
accept our worship of thanksgiving today.

We thank you for the mother earth
   that gives of her bounty to provide for our needs,
for the beauty of your creation
   and all the wonders it contains,
for the gift of life, that which we have lived,
   and for the living of this moment
      and for that life yet to come.

Our desire today, our God,
is that we would be a source of thanksgiving for you.
Delight in us, O Lord,
   as we confess
   our love and gratitude to you,
   our eternal and steadfast God.

As you have blessed us in your love,
   we ask your blessing on others:
bless among us those who are poor in spirit,
   give them your kingdom;
bless those among us who have cause to grieve today,
   give them your comfort;
bless those among us who hunger and thirst to see right prevail,
   may they see your justice on earth;
bless those from among us who show mercy,
   be merciful to them;

bless the peacemakers among us,
   may their way prevail;
bless those who are persecuted for your name's sake
      on this day,
   may they see your kingdom.

And bless the innocent and the powerless,
   those who have no voice in our world.
Make them your own, guard them with your mighty arm.
Be the Lord of hosts for them.
Amen.

WORSHIP

Our ever-present God,
who has dwelt in tabernacles and tents,
who has visited temples and shrines
and has been invited to grace lofty cathedrals
  with your presence,
as we delight in the hints of color in the trees
  that promise a spectacular fall
and as we breathe the cool air
    that frosts the mornings,
  we are reminded that, after all,
  you have no need
    of buildings in which to dwell,
  you have no need
    of shelter from the cold
    or protection from the storm.
For you are our Creator God,
  who plays among the stars
  and delights in the majestic beauty of your creation.

What a wonder then that you would visit us
  in tents and temples,
that you would leave the playfields of the heavens
  to commune with us, your creatures,
    within walls of brick and mortar.
But the greater mystery is that you are content
  to make your home in our hearts.
What a wonder that our bodies carry
  the divine Spirit that makes us one!

Our God, in that oneness of spirit,
  we offer our worship to you,

confessing our corporate yearning
    for your presence,
rejoicing in your gifts of visitation —
    in the colors of the leaves,
    in the uncompromising hugs from our children,
    in kind words of affirmation or sympathy,
    in the sustaining prayers
      of those who love us,
    in the certitude
      of your daily presence.
Amen.

DEAR GOD,
it's Sunday again,
and we find ourselves, again,
    in church, dressed up for worship
    while there is so much else that needs doing.

Some of us are here out of obligation,
some of us found our way here out of habit,
some of us are here out of need.

But it is Sunday again,
    and all of us are here because you have called us
    to be your people and to worship you,
        the only true and living God.

And so, for now, all else waits
    while we sing of your almighty power,
    rejoice in your goodness, confess your loving grace,
    and thank you for the gift of new life
        in Jesus Christ, our Savior.

May our worship today
    be worthy of you.
Amen.

Part Four

PRAYERS FOR
SPECIAL OCCASIONS

T HE SEASONS OF THE CHURCH echo the cosmic cycles of life. Most of us no longer parcel out our time or tasks to the rhythms of the days or cycles of the moon. And in an urban-centered society few of us portion our lives out of the natural cycles of sowing, planting, harvest, and storing. Nonetheless, we seem keenly in touch with that once familiar pulse of life and living. We find comfort and structure in the certain and predictable rotation of holidays, birthdays, and yearly observances.

Giving attention to the seasons and special occasions of the year through corporate prayer is an enriching experience. It affirms that prayer should bathe all aspects of living — from special celebrations to the predictable, sometimes tedious cycles of the seasons. God is in them all.

ALL SAINTS' DAY

Our heavenly Father,
we are filled with anticipation
of fun and frolic on this Halloween Day.
Our children have chosen their costumes for this year:
fairy princesses, ninja turtles, and other characters
we have tolerated with less enthusiasm.
The large candy bowl by the door is ready for the visitation
from other little monsters and ghouls,
heroes and heroines.
And the jack-o'-lantern will be lit as a beacon
announcing their welcome to our doorstep
and, perhaps, as a talisman against
tricks and pranks.
And some of us have exercised great restraint and discipline
in not treating ourselves to the sweets
set aside for our little visitors.

But amid the campy fun,
we are mindful that today is, in fact,
a more solemn day.
Today we think on those called saints,
those from among us who by the examples of their lives
have modeled for us
the best we can hope to be.

Some saints we honor are ancient,
now almost mythic and distant.
But some we have known: fathers and mothers,
brothers and sisters, uncles, aunts, and others
we have known and loved,
who are today not with us in flesh and blood,
(continued)

but certainly in spirit and memory
and in the love that abides still.

We thank you, O God, for the gift
of their presence in our lives.
We thank you for the mark they have left on our souls
and for the legacies of memories, values, and love
they have left for us to enjoy.
Thank you for keeping them in the embrace of your love
and for the rest they have found in your presence.

Help us to live our lives honorably,
to honor them
and to honor you.
Help us to never forget
the best they were able to be
and to forgive their weaknesses and shortcomings
as we ask you also to forgive
our weaknesses and shortcomings.

Accept our gift of worship today
as we offer it in gratitude,
acknowledging that you are
and always will be,
our God.
Amen.

Our God,
from whom all good things come,
who has been our help in all generations,
on the heels of All Saints' Day
we reclaim the moment from the distracting festivities
of costumes, parties, candy, and mischief,
    for its more somber intent:
    to remember the loved ones departed
    who now live in memory's shadows,
    having discarded their bodies
    as clothing out of season.

But despite the great gulf between us,
in your presence they are with us,
    vividly present, advising, admonishing,
    cheering us on, a great cloud of witnesses
        watching over us.
In your love they are more a part of us,
for before we touched body,
    but now our souls are one
    as you are one with us — as you promised.
And in your promises, they eternally live in us,
our memories, our values, our hopes,
    in the semblance of our faces
    and of our children's.

For the hope that sustains,
for the grace that binds,
for the Spirit that empowers,
and for the Savior who reigns,
we give you thanks and praise everlasting.
Amen.

AUTUMN

Our heavenly Father,
our eyes are opened to the beauty of this season.
Around every curve in the road is another explosion
    of fall colors to fill our eyes and delight our souls.
In the light of the October sun the leaves glow
    as bright as a child's watercolor.
And seeing these things, we are able to smile
    and find cause to be grateful.

For the wonder of colors and the gift of sight,
    we thank you.
But our prayer today is not just for sight
    to delight in the beauty of your world,
    but for vision to see your will.

Our God, we beseech you today —
    you who have given us eyes
        to see the light that fills this room —
give us the inward vision
    to behold you in this place.
For this moment, help us raise our sights
    above the mundane,
    help us see beyond the moment.
    Give us a glimpse of your glory,
    an understanding of your eternal perspective,
        and a foretaste of the delight
            of your presence.
Amen.

CHILDREN'S SUNDAY

O̲u̲r̲ G̲o̲d̲,
we take time during our worship of you,
  our God of law and grace,
to celebrate children and this ministry
  to which you have called us.
And we know you do not mind,
for you have taught us
that to such as these does your kingdom belong.

So we thank you today for teachers and caregivers
who hold back the hard edges of life
to preserve the gift of childhood wonderment in our children.

And we thank you for our children,
for the future and the hope
that shines through their thirsty eyes.
For the humbling questions they ask of us:
  Why is the sky blue?
  Why do ducks quack?
  Where do babies come from, and,
    Can I have a little sister?
  Are we rich or are we poor?
  Where does God live?
  And, Do you love me?

Thank you
for the grounding power of their unconditional love
that reminds us
  that it isn't how important we are
  or how smart or how respected by others
  or how successful
  (continued)

that really makes us who we are —
  rather, it is by whom we are loved.

So we confess, our God,
that in the difficult, uncertain times,
  it is enough to be loved by our children
  and by the God who also loves us
  with an infinite, unconditional love
  through the Son who was slain and is now risen,
  Jesus Christ, our Lord.
Amen.

FAMILY

Our God, on this day of family celebrations,
we rejoice in being part of those personal constellations
into which we are born.

Thank you, God, for families,
the persons with whom we share the places we call home,
a refuge from the nameless, uncaring world,
where we recognize ourselves in the faces
of those who share our lives
and in those who have lived before we were given a name
and blessed with a destiny.

Thank you, God, for families that give us a heritage of faith,
that teach us our place in the world
but challenge us to reach beyond ourselves,
that allow us our uniqueness
and celebrate our eccentricities and quirks
by calling us "special."

And thank you, God,
for created families, those of our own choosing,
into which we enter by invitation and adoption,
in which we negotiate our place and calling,
families like church,
which both takes and gives,
blesses and challenges,
and feels just like the place to which we should belong.

And for the holy family,
which birthed and nurtured our Savior
unto that day of destiny,
we give you everlasting praise.
Amen.

FATHER'S DAY

Our Father God,
we thank you today for the fathers in our lives,
for those who by calling or choice,
by virtue of blood or grace,
stand in that place in our lives
and answer the call to be fathers.
Thank you, God,
for perfect daddies, who cradle and cuddle,
who can chase away monsters from under the bed,
who can do anything, it seems,
and who push us toward our place
in a world of possibilities beyond their own reach.

For responsible dads, who provide and protect,
who give up dreams for our sake,
whose form of courage is to face daily
the ordinary task of making a living
and to count personal sacrifices cheap for their families' sake.

For grandfathers whose delight in us is unconditional,
whose patience is endless,
and whose legacy of love and strength
reaches across generations
to give us a past, a name, and a destiny.

And thank you, Father God,
for giving us your name to carry and calling us your own,
for your steadfast love that never fails,
and for making for us a place to call home
from which we have come and to which we return,
always into your loving,
uncompromising embrace.
Amen.

Our God, we celebrate our fathers today,
and our memories and vision for the best they can be:
strong and courageous, gentle and firm,
 heroes of our childhood,
 intolerable in our adolescence,
 and patient, grateful friends in our adulthood.

We thank you for what they have tried to teach us:
 to do the right thing, to be honest and disciplined,
 to try our best no matter the payoff,
 to hit a ball, ride a bike, and catch a fish;
 and for what they have done for us:
 they provided for us as best they could,
 and trusted us with the family car
 (as much as they dared),
 and finally let us go to be our own selves.

And we thank you, God,
that you would choose to call yourself our Father,
and in so doing, you have given us your name,
 and have claimed us as your own,
 and have patiently taught and admonished and protected.

For the orphans of our world —
 created in our foolish, selfish wars,
 through our personal failings
 and our ways contrary to your Spirit of love —
we pray, God our Father,
 that you claim them also as your children,
 that you protect the widow,
 make justice for the poor,
 and give your name to those who are without
 power or voice or hope in our world.
Amen.

FREEDOM

O<small>UR</small> G<small>OD OF</small> L<small>IBERTY</small>,
who has called us to freedom,
we celebrate today the grand experiment of America
   that allows us the freedom to gather
     for the worship of you, our Creator God,
       unhindered except for the unwilling spirit.

We are mindful that this freedom
     was bought with a price,
   and so our celebration is tempered by gratitude
   for the ideologists, the dreamers,
     the patriots, the brave soldiers,
   for all the children and spouses
      who inspired and waited,
     all of whom paid their share in the purchase
      of our freedom.

Our flag flies free again this year
because of your grace, our God,
   and so in gratitude we pray for the freedom
   of those our brothers and sisters
     who live in lands of oppression,
   where even the shadow of your kingdom
     is but a far-distant dream.
We pray for the peoples whose songs
     are not of amber waves of grain
   but of hunger, of desolate lands,
     of abandoned cities
       and war-torn families.

See again the misery of your people in our lands,
hear their crying out because of their oppressors,
    and be again moved by their suffering.

Come down to rescue them from the hand
        of the oppressors of body and spirit,
    and bring them up out of that land
        into a good and spacious land,
    a land flowing with milk and honey —
    the home that is the kingdom of your Son,
        Jesus Christ.
Amen.

FRIENDSHIP

Our God in heaven,
   who is the almighty King,
      but who in your Son now calls us friends,
there are so many people in our lives,
   but, we confess, few in number are they
      whom we call friends,
those who understand why we laugh or cry,
   why we feel downcast for no apparent reason
      and so ask for none,
who accept our changes of mood without telling us
      to "snap out of it,"
   who give us a strong hand and a quiet voice
      when life causes our knees to wobble
      or our hands to shake,
   and who understand the same jokes we do
   and are not afraid to laugh with us,
      even when no one else will.

Bless us, we pray, with more friends who like you,
   see all and say nothing
    — until the right time —
   and then forgive us whether we deserve it or not,
   who celebrate our awkward attempts at success
   because they have high hopes for us,
      even greater than we have for ourselves,
   and in whose comfortable presence
      our loneliness and worry seem to fade.

Our God,
to be such a friend is a sweet and blessed bond, we know,
and so be our friend, we pray, and help us be as friends to you,
faithful and true.
Amen.

                                        Prayers for Special Occasions

INDEPENDENCE DAY

O UR GOD OF FREEDOM,
like the nation of Joshua's Israel of long ago,
our nation was forged by men and women
    of valor and vision.
On this long weekend of rest and play,
    of barbecues, baseball games, and picnics,
    we celebrate your gift of liberty.

By your grace, this year again,
    our nation's flag flies over a land
        of freedom and abundance,
And so we pray for the peoples in this world
    who this year have no flag to salute,
    whose hunger, fear, and uncertainty leave no room
        for feelings of patriotism.

By your grace, this year again,
we worship as we choose and where we want.
And so we pray for our sisters and brothers
    whose liberty is denied,
    who pray in whispers and meet in secret,
    who hunger for your spoken Word,
    and who wear on their bodies
    the scars that mark them as your children.

By your grace, this year again,
    our children will delight in night skies
        blazoned by fireworks.
And so we pray for those corners in our land
    where light seems never to lessen the darkness,
    where poverty kills the spirit
    (continued)

and bigotry demeans the person
and hatred is a badge;
where children go hungry still
and adults find no hope
for an American dream.

And by your grace, this year again,
we pray that you spare us and our own from these,
and in so doing call us, like Joshua,
to claim our land in your name
and fight your fight of justice,
that your name may be established in our land.
Amen.

MEMORIAL

Our heavenly Father,
we have gathered for these few minutes to quietly remember
some who have become dear to us.

We have been privileged to have been welcomed
    into their homes
and in some cases welcomed into "family."
That honor is not lost on us, knowing that we have been blessed
    by that gracious acceptance.

We were called upon to bring comfort where there was pain,
    to bring peace where there was anxiety,
    to bring assurance where there was loneliness and fear,
    to offer hope where there was none.

Our God,
we were privileged to witness the lives of families
    that embraced and protected in times of trouble.
We have seen the steadfast love that comes
    from years of companionship.
We have been surprised by that personal strength
    with which you have gifted each of us,
a strength that can bear all things — even unto death.

We think of our friends and their families
    with a sense of gratitude,
    and in so thinking, we honor them.
For surely just as we touched their bodies with our hands,
    they have touched our spirits and left a mark.
They have taught us to be gracious
    even in times of personal discomfort.
    (continued)

They have given us the gift of laughter
   that transcends tribulations.
They have shared treasured life stories
   that enable us to be a little wiser if we've listened.
They have made us feel wanted and needed and important —
   and that is a rare gift in today's world.
Most importantly, perhaps, they have allowed us
   to learn to give of our ourselves,
   to face the inevitable loss,
   to love a little better.

Our prayer this day is for peace for them
and healing for their families.
Amen.

MOTHER'S DAY

Our God,
we have set aside the sabbath day to worship you,
    for you alone are worthy of our devotion.

But we've set aside *this* day for our mothers, too,
    and we know you don't mind,
    for they embody your grace in ways
    that give us cause
        to worship you more deeply.

They give us life;
    they sustain us in our dependency
    and guard us in our vulnerability.
Mothers forgive us, no matter what,
    but they can lead us to repentance
        with one knowing look.
Mothers love us like no one else ever will
    and teach volumes about life by their example:
    to wash our hands before eating,
    to put on our sweaters before going out,
        to scrub behind our ears.
    They teach us that we can do
        what we set our hearts to accomplish,
    that we are never really alone in this life,
        and that no matter how big we get,
            we can always go home.

Our mothers' love is like yours, O God,
    and nothing could be deeper or purer
        or more redeeming.
Thank you, God, for our mothers,
    and may your name be praised.
        Amen.

SENIOR ADULTS

Our God, ancient of days,
who dwells in the most high
    but can yet hear our prayers of worship and cries for help,
we honor today those in our community
whom you've blessed with the gift of time and long life.

We celebrate the noble symbols
    of having lived and struggled
    and taken on life on its own terms:
    the snowy crown, experienced hands,
    and the lines that map faces marking years of laughter,
    revealing the character of wisdom,
a friendly acquaintance with sorrow and pain,
and the learned patience that all things come in their time.
The smile that hints of having learned that life
is an unpredictable mixture of blessing and grief
    made up of dreams realized
        through sacrifice, hope, and work,
and of disappointment reminding us
    that this is a far from perfect world,
    but that life is, after all, good
    and your most precious gift to us.

For their lives and their example
    to us who have yet to travel the roads they've trod,
for their investment of self and time
    that have shaped our community,
and for their legacy of faith that will make our way
    easier and richer and nobler, we praise you.

Bless them we pray, and give the angels charge over them
    to guard their ways all the days of their lives.
Amen.

STEWARDSHIP

Our Creator God,
maker of heaven and earth
and Lord of life,
in these good days we thank you for the eyes of faith,
    for they allow us to see the invisible
        but really *real* things in our lives.
Through the eyes of faith we can see in a love
unlimited by the paltry colors of the human spectrum,
    and in your gift of boundless grace
    we find freedom to grow and to give
    beyond the limitations of our boldest dreams.

We thank you for the intangibles:
for the coinage in our life
    that remains hidden until it pays dividends —
    discipline and justice and loyalty to truth,
        friendships and commitment
            and faith.

Help us, our God,
    to put our treasures where our hearts should be,
    so that in desiring the eternal things
        of greater value,
    we can hold life loosely
        and treasure it as that greatest gift of grace
            from you, our Creator God.
Amen.

SUMMER

Our Creator God,
we are grateful this morning for summertime,
for lazy days of vacation and re-creation,
for days of leisure that allow us to remove ourselves
    from the workaday world,
for the chance to watch children at play,
    energized by the sunshine,
    reminding us that life, above all else, is to be enjoyed.

We thank you for the getting-away-from-it-all days
    that allow us to get a new perspective on the gift of work,
for the chance to be reminded that our toil is not
    an adamic curse
but an affirmation of our worth,
    a working out of our calling,
    and a participation in your work of creation.
May these days of respite from work —
    whether we run the machine, mold the vision,
    count the parts, check the numbers, place the orders,
    build the towers, heal the body, feed the mind,
    or care for the spirit —
serve to remind us that it is through our work
    that you have called us to join you
        in the redeeming of your world.

And remind us
when we walk barefoot in the grass,
    or stand in the froth of the ocean,
    or lick the dripping ice cream from between our fingers,
    or lie back in awe of the countless stars in the summer sky,
that you remain our God of joy and fun and laughter,
that you are our God of re-creation.
Amen.

OUR GOD OF REST AND WORK, Creator of seasons,
thank you for the fading summer.

Thank you for distractions from routine,
   for respite from work and worries.
Thank you for the chances to "get away"
   that allow distance from the irksome peccadilloes
   that nag our consciences and bleed our energies,
      distance that allows fresh perspectives,
      renewed creativity,
      and a fresh commitment to work and play.

Thank you for Bible schools and summer camps and new friends,
   for parks and swimming pools,
   for ponds teeming with tadpoles
   and squirmy polliwogs and salamanders,
      for the homesickness that reminds us
      of where our heart is,
      and for memories enough for a lifetime.

And thank you, God, for vacations,
   too hectic and too expensive,
   too hot and too commercial... and too short,
but in the end, always bringing us back to better places:
   home where we belong,
   to the vocations that define us,
      and to the people who love us
      and call us their own.

Our God, as the summer fades
   and we turn to busy ourselves with school and work,
   send your Spirit to give us pause to praise you,
      our God of the renewing seasons.
Amen.

THANKSGIVING DAY

OUR GOD,
giver of life, provider of all good things from above,
we gather to sing of your blessings.

We anticipate the celebration of Thanksgiving Day.
We will enjoy a rest from our work
    to delight in the company of family and guests.
We will celebrate with good food and drink
    and enjoy the chaos of children underfoot
    and relax as we talk and watch ball games
    and wait to make room
        for one more piece of pie.

But for the moment,
    we gather to enjoy one another's company in fellowship
    with these who are friends and family —
    there are no "guests" here
        in your house of worship.
We pause to examine our privileged lives,
    to wonder at the happy accidents
        of good fortune in our lives,
    to contemplate how your providential hand
        has guided us throughout this year,
        guarding, guiding,
        blessing us in ways too numerous to count,
        protecting us in ways unseen and unsuspected.

We thank you, our God, for your gift of life,
but more, for the gift of new life in your Son, Jesus Christ.
Accept our expressions of gratitude,
    for they come from the heart.
Amen.

OUR GOD IN HEAVEN, we, your thankful people,
   have gathered to sing and voice our gratitude
      in this Thanksgiving season.

We thank you for all the blessings of the year,
   for times of health
   when we've been free from pain and discomfort,
   when our bodies worked
      according to your masterful design.

We thank you for the privilege of living here,
   in this corner of the globe,
   where we have been free from war and pestilence and want,
   where our children are not hungry or cold or unloved;
   may it be ever so.

We thank you for the provision of friends and family
      and community —
   those who have sustained us and supported us,
      who have believed in us and encouraged us
      and challenged us to be the person you intended us to be.

We thank you for the illnesses
   that made us count on your sustaining grace,
   for the death that freed from senseless pain,
   for the failures that made us wiser,
   for the trials that made us stronger,
   and for the disappointments that, in the end,
      made us look to *you*.

But we thank you, above all, for the gift of life itself,
   for the mystery of being and thinking and feeling and loving,
   and for our *new* life in our Savior, Jesus Christ.
Amen.

OUR GOD,
the times they are a-changing.
It used to be so simple to mark the season, it seems.
But today, pity the parent who is to teach the child
    in the supermarket stroller
    about times and seasons:
    Is it Thanksgiving or Christmas?
And whatever happened to Advent?

Well, it's Thanksgiving time,
and so in practiced postures
we express our gratitude
    for the life of our making.

But our confession, O God,
is that genuine gratitude is often hard for us,
    for we are also gifted with self-sufficiency,
    with the means to choose our way.
Affluence in our country
    is the ability to buy space.
It is to have the wherewithal to protect ourselves
    and our loved ones from ... "others,"
really, to distance ourselves
    from the harsher realities of our world
    that define the lives of peripheral people
    who hunger
    and despair
    and live out the darker side
    of the American dream.

God, our feelings of gratitude are so often
    just pangs of relief

that we and ours are blessed
    and spared.

May your blessings of talents and wealth
    never separate us from our sisters and brothers
    who share in the same hope
    that in our better moments brings us to our knees
    in true gratitude:
    the gift of new life
        in your Son, Jesus Christ.

In this Thanksgiving season,
teach us gratitude, our God.
Amen.

Index of Themes